2-18

URBAN LEGENDS

Close Encounters

C.M. Johnson

full tilt PRESS

Close Encounters

Origins: Urban Legends

Full Tilt Press
42982 Osgood Road
Fremont, CA 94539

Full Tilt Press publications may be purchased for educational, business, or sales promotional use.

Editorial Credits
Design and layout by Sara Radka
Edited by Lauren Dupuis-Perez
Copyedited by Renae Gilles

Image Credits
Getty Images: iStockphoto, cover, 4, 14, 24, 28, 34, 36, 37, 38; NASA, 20, 43; Newscom: Alex Milan Tracy/NurPhoto/
Sipa U, 40, Blend Images LLC, 23, dpa/picture-alliance, 33, 30, Moore Mike Mirrorpix, 31, Werner Forman, 13;
Shutterstock: Astanin, 27, Dan Breckwoldt, 11, Danita Delmont, 10, Denis Belitsky, 44, Herbert Eisengruber, 7, Jarno
Gonzalez Zarraonandia, 6, lassedesignen, 17, Litwin Photography, 25, M. Cornelius, 16, Marcel Jancovic, 26, Mette
Fairgrieve, 41, rayints, 8, Rommel Canlas, 15, roundstripe, 21, Stocksnapper, 18, Vecteezy, 46, cover and background
elements; Wikimedia: Liangent, 35

ISBN: 978-1-62920-611-0 (library binding)
ISBN: 978-1-62920-623-3 (eBook)

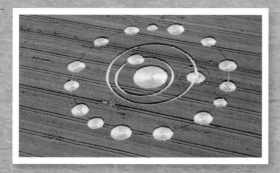

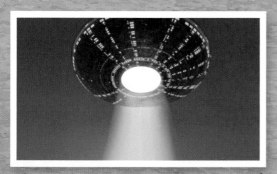

CONTENTS

ANCIENT ALIENS

Some people believe aliens built great works around the world, like the statues found on Rapa Nui, an island in the South Pacific Ocean.

INTRODUCTION

How were the pyramids built? Why did early cultures draw people with huge heads? Where did the Greeks get a myth about a sky god who gave people the gift of fire? Some say that aliens from other planets are the answer. They think aliens came to Earth long ago. Some people believe aliens did **genetic engineering** on primates that helped apes evolve into humans.

Other people think the aliens gave us tools and big ideas. Maybe aliens told us about math. Maybe they gave us maps of the stars. Some people even believe the theory that humans are aliens. They think aliens came to Earth when their own planet died. Maybe they began a new life here, and we are their **descendants**. Is there evidence in art, myth, and **architecture** that aliens were once among us? If so, why did they come here? And will they ever come back?

genetic engineering: cutting up and combining genetic material from two different species in order to produce certain traits in a new plant or animal

descendant: a person who is related by blood to a common ancestor

architecture: the art and science of building things

Some of the animal and plant shapes on the Nazca desert are as long as the Empire State Building is tall.

BEST RECORDED SIGHTING

In the early 1900s, the first planes began to fly over Peru. While flying over a region near Nazca, pilots noticed something odd. On the red and tan desert ground, they saw strips of white. The marks formed 800 straight lines and 300 shapes. Some of these were **geometric** shapes, such as triangles. There were also 70 plant and animal designs. The marks could be seen only from the sky. They went on for miles (kilometers).

geometric: based on simple shapes like circles, lines, or squares

Scientists began to study the lines. The Nazca people had made them 500 to 2,000 years ago. They had scraped the red dirt from the surface to reveal the pale sand beneath. This area in Peru gets very little wind and rain. That is why the lines stayed intact. But why had people made shapes they could not even see? Writers such as Erich von Däniken came up with an idea. He noted that some of the straight lines ran up to 30 miles (48 kilometers) long. He thought the lines could be landing strips for alien ships. Had aliens told people how to make the designs? Or had the aliens made the lines themselves?

drought: a period of time in which not enough rain falls to keep plants and animals healthy

The Nazca lines cover hundreds of square miles (kilometers) between the towns of Nazca and Palpa in Peru.

TIMELINE

Historical myths and legends may show evidence of aliens visiting Earth.

10,000 BC
People in the area of modern-day Italy draw what look like astronaut suits.

40,000 BC
Early people in Australia tell a story about "sky-beings." They came to earth to create people.

2589–2532 BC
The Great Pyramids of Giza are built in Egypt.

1352 BC
Akhenaten takes the throne in Egypt. Drawings of him show that he had a very long skull.

AD 500–600
The intricate stone structures called Puma Punku are built in the area of modern-day Bolivia.

1970

Two members of the Soviet Academy of Sciences come up with a theory about the moon. They say it may actually be an ancient alien ship.

1968

Erich von Däniken publishes his book *Chariots of the Gods?* Many people hear about ancient alien theories for the first time.

1974

Claude Vorilhon starts an ancient alien religion called Raëlism.

1956

Morris K. Jessup publishes his book *UFO and the Bible*. He says that the story about Jesus rising up to heaven was most likely describing a spaceship beaming him up.

2015

The Big Questions television show debates whether or not major religious figures were aliens.

Each pyramid was built as a tribute to a pharaoh, or king. The Egyptians believed their pharaohs were chosen by gods in the sky.

EVIDENCE FOR AND AGAINST

The Great Pyramid of Khufu amazes engineers. It is very large. Each side is about 750 feet (229 meters) long. It is almost 500 feet (152 m) tall. The pyramid is made of more than two million stone blocks. It is lined up with the points of the **compass**. Some say that people from early times could not have made it. Maybe aliens helped them. How could humans have lifted the heavy blocks by themselves? They did not yet have machines. Even though the Egyptians lived long ago, their brains were the same as our own. Historians say that Egyptians were curious and smart. They say the Egyptians hauled the blocks on ramps made of earth and wood. No one knows for sure.

compass: a device for determining direction

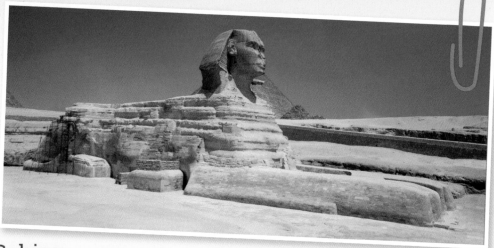

Sphinx

Near the Great Pyramids in Egypt is another great **marvel**. This is the stone Sphinx. The Sphinx has the head of a man and the body of a lion. It is 66 feet (20 m) tall and 240 feet (73 m) long. Its paws are about as long as an 18-wheeler. The statue was carved from a single piece of rock. In myths, the Sphinx is often both wise and cruel. The creature tells clever riddles. If people cannot answer correctly, they are **devoured**.

In America, the Algonquian native people tell a myth about a "sky girl." She liked each of her homes, one on Earth and the other in the sky. She moved back and forth between them. She liked to learn about the animals on the Earth. Is the sky girl based on aliens who went from our planet to another one on a ship? Were aliens curious about people and other animals? Myths of "sky people" are found all over the world. Humans have always had wild imaginations, but some people say there must be a reason that so many cultures tell similar stories.

marvel: something that inspires surprise and amazement

devoured: eaten up greedily

Is It Out There?

Why were the Nazca lines made on the ground of Peru? Professor Paul Kosok said the lines might make up a calendar. Other scientists think they were trails that led to **sacred** spaces. People may have prayed in these spaces. They may have asked the gods for rain.

Do these ideas disprove the possibility of aliens being involved? Some people say that aliens and their technology gave rise to our belief in gods. Think of early humans looking up at the sky. They have never seen a machine. They have not yet used electricity. The glow of an alien ship appears. Unlike a star, it comes closer. Today, we might say it was a plane or a drone. To ancient people, magic would have been the only answer. Were the Nazca praying to aliens, whether they knew it or not?

Why does the pharaoh Akhenaten's head have a long shape? Doctors think it could be from a birth defect. This defect causes the bones of the skull to close before the brain is fully formed. As a baby's brain grows, the head takes on a long shape. People who say they have seen real aliens think the pharaoh's skull shape is not from a birth defect. They say Akhenaten's long head matches the shape of the aliens they've seen. Could an alien race have ruled ancient Egypt? If so, could their descendants have visited Earth in modern times?

sacred: something that is respected for being holy or used to pray to a god or gods

Are statues of the unusual-looking Akhenaten evidence that he was an alien ruler from another planet?

DUCTIONS

...e report seeing blinding lights right
...are beamed up into a ship in the sky.

INTRODUCTION

A woman lies in her bed at night. An eerie feeling comes over her. Suddenly, there are creatures in the room. They walk on two legs like humans, but their heads are large. Their skin is gray or green. They take her onto a ship and perform tests on her as if she were a science experiment. The tests seem to go on for hours. But when she finds herself back in bed, only a few minutes have passed.

A man is out driving. He sees an odd light in the sky. A beam shoots down to earth. It sucks him up into an alien ship, where he goes through the same **ordeal** as the woman. Millions of people say they have been **abducted** by aliens, and most of their stories are similar. The stories began to be reported in the late 1800s. Is this when aliens began to arrive?

Do aliens sneak into houses at night and steal people away while they are half-asleep?

DID YOU KNOW?
In 2014, a British talk show conducted a survey. They found that 1 in 25 people believed that they had been abducted by aliens.

ordeal: a difficult or unpleasant experience

abducted: to be taken somewhere against your will

Were aliens looking for people to study, deep in the woods of Arizona?

BEST RECORDED SIGHTING

In November of 1975, Arizona logger Travis Walton was heading home with his crew. It had been a long day out in the Apache-Sitgreaves National Forest. The men say that all of a sudden, a glowing yellow disk appeared in the sky. They followed it down a dirt road. When they were close, they saw that the light was a spaceship. Walton got out of the truck. The ship made some beeps and rumbles. He got closer, and it began to move. Then a blue-green ray threw him 10 or 20 feet (3 to 6 m) into the air. Sure he was dead, the other loggers fled in terror. They later returned to help him. But when they got there, Walton was gone.

Walton was missing for five days. The police suspected **foul play**. They questioned his friends. Then Walton turned up several miles (kilometers) away. He said that after the blast, he woke up on a table on the alien ship. Small beings with big brown eyes were leaning over him. They wore orange surgical gowns. Walton's shirt had been pulled up, exposing his chest and stomach. Terrified, he batted at the aliens with his hands. Their bodies felt soft and spongy. Finally, they left him. Walton blacked out. Later, he woke up in a gas station. He did not know how much time had passed.

foul play: criminal violence or dishonest acts

UFO: an Unidentified Flying Object

Travis Walton says his logging buddies yelled at him to come back to the truck right before he was hit by a beam from a UFO.

TIMELINE

Alien abductions have been reported all over the world throughout modern history.

1946
"Planet Comics" runs a strip in which aliens beam up a young woman.

1896
In Lodi, California, Colonel H.G. Shaw says he and a friend fought off three tall aliens. He claims that the aliens flew off in a ship.

1957
A young man in Brazil says that he met a pretty female alien onboard a UFO.

1961
Betty and Barney Hill claim that while driving in rural New Hampshire, they were taken by aliens in dark jackets.

1976

Four fishermen in Maine claim a UFO beamed them up with their canoe.

1993

The movie *Fire in the Sky* is based on Travis Walton's experience in Arizona.

1971

Israeli illusionist Uri Geller says that, at the age of three, he met alien beings. He says they gave him psychic powers.

2010

Russian politician Kirsan Ilyumzhinov says aliens told him that the game of chess was brought to Earth from outer space.

In the 1960s, American President John F. Kennedy (right) pushed for the nation to become the first to send a person to the moon.

Evidence For and Against

Why did stories of abductions begin in the late 1800s? Why did the number of stories hit a **peak** in the 1950s and '60s? Right before 1900, people flew the first airships and airplanes. Rockets were soon to follow. In 1961, the first human went into space. Writers and artists began to wonder if beings from other planets were going into space, too. They drew flying **saucers** in books and comic strips. They wrote about lights that beamed people up. These details then showed up in stories of "real" alien encounters. Is this why people's stories are similar? Did comic strips prompt dreams that seemed real?

peak: the highest point

saucer: a small plate

Like Travis Walton, some people have written books about their alien stories. They sell the stories to magazines. They sell the movie rights. Did Walton make up his story for money? Walton says no. He also says he has a way to prove his story. Trees near the area of his abduction grew faster than usual in the years after he was taken. Did **radiation** from the ship cause the change? In a video, Walton points to tree rings that seem to prove his point. Without scientific studies to back him up, we can't know for sure. Was the growth due to a natural cause? Or is Walton right?

radiation: energy put off in waves or particles

Reading Rings

A tree stump is covered with concentric circles called rings. Concentric circles share the same central point. A tree's rings can tell us what has happened to it over time. Each spring, the tree adds a new layer of wood to its trunk. The distance between a circle and the one next to it

shows how much the tree grew that year. A thick ring might mean a year with lots of rain. A thin ring might mean the tree had many trees around it competing for sun. Fires and damage from insects can also be "read" in the rings of a tree.

Is It Out There?

Police officers and doctors often study people who say they have met with aliens. They try to figure out if a person is telling the truth. The people take lie detector tests. Doctors look for signs of **psychosis**. If the person is not lying or mentally ill, does that mean the story must be real? Doctors say not necessarily. Most accounts of abductions are not told right after the event. Instead, a person has bad dreams. They are vivid and scary. They disrupt a person's sleep. That person might seek help to get rid of the dreams. Under hypnosis, they "remember" an abduction. Is it a memory of a real event? Or is it a memory of the dream? Doctors say it is hard to know for sure.

> **DID YOU KNOW?**
> Under hypnosis, Israeli illusionist Uri Geller said that aliens told him that the nation of Israel was under special **cosmic** protection.

psychosis: a mental condition in which a person cannot tell what is real from what is not

cosmic: relating to the whole universe

What evidence is needed to prove the stories are real? Maybe one day, scientists will find an unearthly device put into a person's body. Maybe a person will grab a piece of an alien ship and bring it back. These items would also offer clues as to what the aliens were up to. What might their technology be like? What might they want to know about us?

Some **people** say **they have** been visited or **taken** by **aliens many** times during their lives, starting when they were children.

CROP CIRCLES

Crop circles are often first seen from a nearby hill or from a plane.

INTRODUCTION

One night, a field of wheat is just a field of wheat. The next morning, it is a work of art. Some of the stalks have been flattened into a shape. There might be a perfect circle, or many circles. There might be a complex pattern, such as the shape of birds. These patterns are usually called crop circles. Most of the circles are in Great Britain, but in recent years they have spread all over the world. The patterns have also become more elaborate. When word gets out that a crop circle has been found, people flock to the site. They come up with ideas about who, or what, might have made the circles. Was it a small whirlwind, called a dust devil? Was it the activity of some **nocturnal** animal? Or could it be aliens? Maybe the circular spot marks the place where a flying saucer landed. Or maybe the patterns are a message from outer space.

Sometimes crop circles are so perfect, it is hard to imagine them being made by animals or the wind.

nocturnal: active mostly at night

domesticated: a plant or animal taken from the wild and adapted for human use

Were the circles people saw the impressions of a flying saucer that touched down on the ground?

BEST RECORDED SIGHTING

On April 6, 1966, more than two hundred people saw something in the sky. It was the middle of the day. Students and staff at two schools in Westall, Australia, looked up to see a UFO. It **hovered** for 20 minutes. It was silver and shaped like a saucer. One man said it was the size of two cars. The craft landed behind some pine trees. Then it took off again and was gone. When people ran to the spot where they had seen it land, they said they found circles in the grass. Some said it looked like the grass had been flattened or **scorched**.

hover: to hang in the air for a period of time

scorch: to burn a surface to the point that its color and texture change

Local papers ran some of the eyewitness accounts. They said that local police and the Royal Australian Air Force were looking into it. They also said that many people were asked by the police to keep quiet. Some said that officials burned the "landing site." In 2005, a professor named Shane Ryan began to dig into the story. He talked to witnesses. He studied the many news accounts. He looked into Air Force and police reports. He wanted to find pictures of the circles. But he said the Air Force told him they had never heard of it. Were they trying to cover up the event? If so, why?

Some people think the burned ground in Westall, Australia, was caused by police and military officers destroying evidence of a secret government project.

TIMELINE

Crop circles are not a new phenomenon. But their purpose remains a mystery.

1678

An English woodcut shows Satan cutting circles into a field with a scythe.

1600s

The first crop circles appear in English fields.

1686

British scientist Robert Plot says the circles might be caused by airflows.

1966

Near Tully, Australia, a farmer says he saw a flying saucer rise into the sky. He finds a circle of flattened grass he says was made by the ship.

1970s

Simple crop circles begin to appear in Wiltshire, England. The number of circles hits a peak in the 1980s.

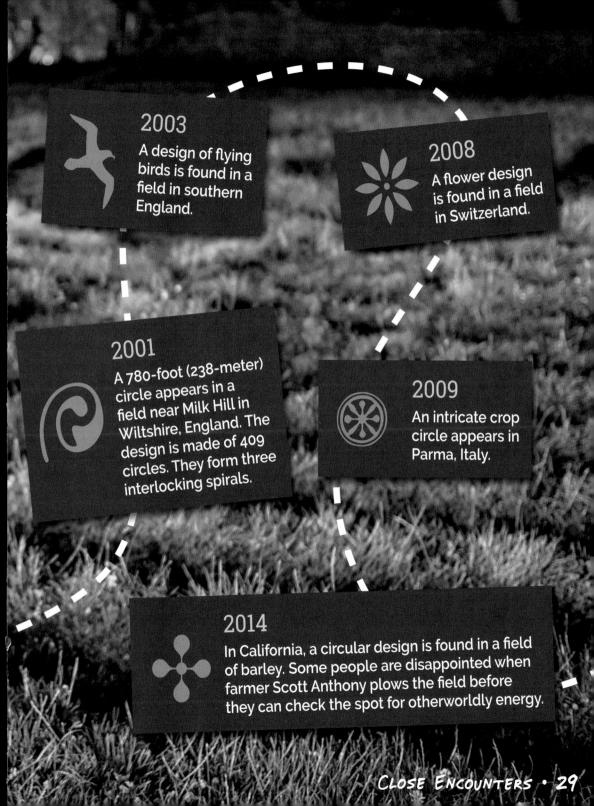

2003
A design of flying birds is found in a field in southern England.

2008
A flower design is found in a field in Switzerland.

2001
A 780-foot (238-meter) circle appears in a field near Milk Hill in Wiltshire, England. The design is made of 409 circles. They form three interlocking spirals.

2009
An intricate crop circle appears in Parma, Italy.

2014
In California, a circular design is found in a field of barley. Some people are disappointed when farmer Scott Anthony plows the field before they can check the spot for otherworldly energy.

Doug Bower showed reporters how he and Dave Chorley made crop circles with their wooden "stompers."

EVIDENCE FOR AND AGAINST

Do humans make the crop circles? In 1991, two painters in Warminster, England, said yes. Doug Bower and Dave Chorley had been making circles since 1976. They showed how they had done it. Their trick was inspired by the UFO reports in Australia. The men even joined in on investigations. They told people they'd been birdwatching when they found new circles. But they actually made the circles themselves. They had fun listening to theories about hedgehogs and ghosts.

Designing Crop Circles

To make a crop circle, Bower would first draft a design at home. On a fine summer night, he and Dave Chorley would go out to a field. They stomped stalks down with a plank of wood threaded on each end with a rope. In 1985, Bower's wife began to suspect something. She saw that the **odometer** on her husband's car was high. Where was he driving to at night? When Bower told her the truth, she did not believe him. He told her to design a crop circle and give it to him. Soon, her design was in a nearby field.

Some "cereologists" did not believe them. These are people who study crop circles. They said the men could not have made the circles so fast. And how had they not left tracks in or out of the field? Bower and Chorley said they had just walked carefully. But they did say they had not made all the circles. Who made the others? Was it other artists? Were the artists from this planet or another one? Had aliens sent down energy beams to make the art? Some people say the circles are filled with healing energy. In 1997, a woman named Stace Tussel felt sick. Then she stepped into a crop circle in Bishops Cannings, England. Her illness went away.

odometer: a device that measures a distance traveled

Is It Out There?

Most farmers do not like crop circles. The damage can mean lost money. People who come out to take a look crush the crops as well. They ask a lot of questions, and keep farmers from getting to their work. Richard Taylor is the director of the Materials Science Institute at the University of Oregon. He says that crop circles have gone high tech. The artists seem to be using **GPS** and lasers. They use microwave generators. Taylor does not worry about whether the artists are alien or human. He does worry that the microwaves could affect the safety of our food.

The new crop circles are often **dazzling**. In 2009, a 600-foot (183-m) jellyfish appeared in Oxfordshire, England. Other fields feature human faces. People get excited when a new circle pops up. They talk about how it might have been made. Many people go see it and share stories about what they felt there. They ask what will come next. But all of the **hype** can make us forget where this all began. The circles in Australia in the 1960s were simple. But people who saw them saw odd aircraft, too. Did the Australian Air Force make these ships? Were the aircraft part of a secret project? Or were they not of this earth?

GPS: a Global Positioning System, used to find a location

dazzling: something that impresses with its beauty or brilliance

hype: excessive promotion or publicity

Should we worry that someone or something is stomping all over crops that later end up as our food?

When people see an unmoving light in the sky, but it is not a star or a planet, it is often hard to say what it could be.

INTRODUCTION

Until we know what it is, any object in the sky is an Unidentified Flying Object. An odd light or shape might turn out to be a plane. It might be a **satellite**. It might be a big bird. Or could it be an alien ship? In 1947, a pilot saw some bright objects while he was flying in Washington state. The objects were weaving in and out of the mountains. They were shaped like **boomerangs**. The pilot said they moved like a saucer being skipped over water, and the term "flying saucer" was born. Alien ships shaped like disks were soon in comic strips. They showed up in movies. The US Air Force became interested in UFOs, too. In 1948, they began a study on aliens that came to be known as Project Blue Book. If aliens were here, they wanted to know about it.

The Madonna with Saint Giovannino hangs in the Palazzo Vecchio Museum in Florence, Italy.

satellite: an object or vehicle made to orbit the Earth or moon

boomerang: a V-shaped toy or weapon that returns to its thrower if it misses its target

Could alien ships have energy beams strong enough to pick up a 500-pound (230-kilogram) calf?

BEST RECORDED SIGHTING

Seeing a UFO is often an **uncanny** experience. In some cases, the weirdness does not end there. In July of 2009, Manuel Sanchez began to see blue lights above a ridge on his ranch in southern Colorado. He did not know why the lights were there. Not long after, he made a creepy discovery. Something was killing his calves, and it did not look like coyotes. The calves had been skinned. Their organs and udders had been removed as if by a surgeon. Their tongues were gone. But there was no blood on the ground. Sanchez called the police and a veterinarian, who were **baffled**. They said no animal could have done it. It must have been humans. But how did people get to the calves? There were no footprints or vehicle tracks.

uncanny: something that feels mysterious or supernatural

baffled: completely puzzled or confused

Another rancher named Tom Miller reported a similar case. A cattle expert came out to look at his dead calf. He could not explain the laser-like cuts. He also said it looked like the calf had been dropped from a tall height. It had many broken bones. Did aliens beam up the calf and take its parts to study? Did they drop it from the sky when they were done?

In western states like Colorado and New Mexico, thousands of cows, horses, and even elk have been killed in the same eerie way as Manuel Sanchez's calves. In almost every case, the killer remains a mystery.

TIMELINE

Sightings of alien spacecrafts have been reported worldwide since the 1890s.

1947

A flying saucer crash is reported on a ranch near Roswell, New Mexico.

1897

The *Dallas Morning News* reports the crash of a UFO that left a dead alien.

1952

Unexplained aircraft and a white substance called "angel hair" that covers the ground are both seen in Oloron, France.

1959

Scientists at a university in Portugal collect and study "angel hair." They find it is a vegetable product.

2001

The British Flying Saucer Bureau says it is shutting down due to a lack of recent sightings.

1997

Hundreds of people in Arizona and New Mexico see a string of lights that form a V shape in the sky.

2009

Groups of red lights move silently over Morris County, New Jersey. They vanish one by one. This is later found to be a hoax.

1969

The US Air Force ends Project Blue Book. They say they have found no evidence of alien ships.

2012

A video taken from a plane shows what looks like a white oval object flying over Seoul, South Korea.

Some people believe the metallic materials found near Roswell, New Mexico, were parts of a balloon. Others believe they were evidence of an alien ship.

EVIDENCE FOR AND AGAINST

Most people who spot lights or objects in the sky are not scientists or pilots. When they try to identify an object, they might not know what they are looking for. Many UFOs turn out to be ordinary things when the right person sees them. An odd shape turns out to be a weather balloon. The red lights in New Jersey were a hoax. Two kids had tied road flares to balloons.

Weather Balloons

Twice a day, all around the world, about 800 weather balloons are sent high above the Earth. They carry instruments that measure things like temperature and **humidity**. These instruments are called the "scientific payload" of the balloon. The balloon is filled with helium. This is a gas that rises because it is less dense than air. When the balloon bursts at the edge of space, the payload comes back to the Earth under a parachute.

The US Air Force says they have never found an alien craft. That is why they ended Project Blue Book. But many alien **conspiracy theorists** do not believe them. These people say alien bodies are kept at Area 51, an Air Force base in Nevada. They do not believe the official report that says the crash in Roswell, New Mexico, was of a spy balloon. They cite the testimony of Major Jesse Marcel. Marcel said he was at the crash site. He said he found odd materials there. He spoke about a type of wood that could be bent, but not burnt. There was also metal as thin as tin foil. It weighed almost nothing, yet it could not be dented with a hammer. Were these materials not of this world?

humidity: the level of moisture in the air

conspiracy theorist: a person who explains an event as the result of a secret plot, usually put together by powerful people

Is It Out There?

Are governments hiding what they know about aliens? Why might they do so? Many people get ideas about what aliens are like from movies. The creature in *Alien* is vicious. In *Invasion of the Body Snatchers*, aliens make creepy copies of people. Would people panic if they knew aliens were here? Is the Air Force trying to keep us calm?

Not all movie aliens are mean. In *E.T.*, an alien is a boy's best friend. The creatures in *Close Encounters of the Third Kind* want to share ideas. Engineer Joseph A. Angelo, Jr. says that most ideas about aliens do not give them much credit. Why would aliens pop down to Earth to scare one person or kill a cow? Space travel is difficult. Angelo says that aliens who had created the technology to get here would be very smart. They would be able to study us from far away. And if aliens did want to see us up close, why not land in a city? Why not find **astronomers** and **astrophysicists** to talk to? What might we learn about the universe if that meeting happens one day?

NASA: the National Aeronautics and Space Administration

astronomer: someone who studies the physical properties of objects and matter outside Earth's atmosphere

astrophysicist: a type of astronomer who studies the behavior and processes of objects in space

The "Golden Record" NASA sent into space for aliens to find contains the sounds of birds, wind, and thunder.

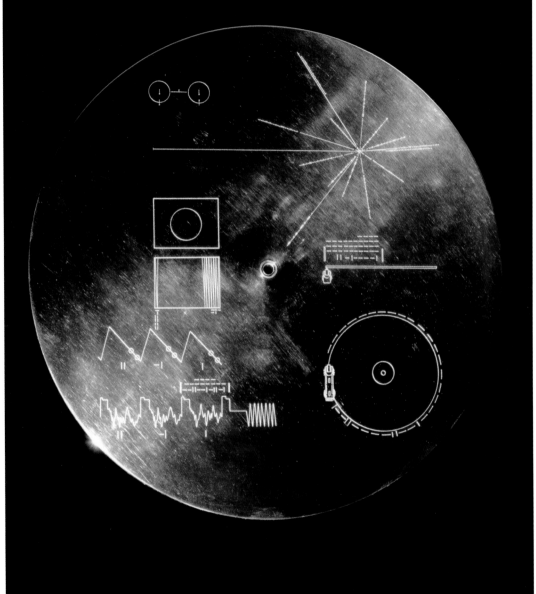

CONCLUSION

Do aliens exist? Life has been on Earth for billions of years. Simple forms have evolved into complex ones. What might be happening on other planets?

Carl Sagan was a 20th-century scientist. He did not think UFOs were alien ships. He did not think aliens would look like humans. Still, he thought that alien life was likely. Our galaxy is one of hundreds of billions of others. Our planet is just a speck in all that space. And, he said, "The stuff of life is everywhere." Sagan thought aliens might try to reach us one day. He also said aliens would most likely be very advanced. What might aliens be able to teach us?

GLOSSARY

abducted: to be taken somewhere against your will

architecture: the art and science of building things

astronomer: someone who studies the physical properties of objects and matter outside Earth's atmosphere

astrophysicist: a type of astronomer who studies the behavior and processes of objects in space

baffled: completely puzzled or confused

boomerang: a V-shaped toy or weapon that returns to its thrower if it misses its target

compass: a device for determining direction

conspiracy theorist: a person who explains an event as the result of a secret plot, usually put together by powerful people

cosmic: relating to the whole universe

dazzling: something that impresses with its beauty or brilliance

descendant: a person who is related by blood to a common ancestor

devoured: eaten up greedily

domesticated: a plant or animal taken from the wild and adapted for human use

drought: a period of time in which not enough rain falls to keep plants and animals healthy

foul play: criminal violence or dishonest acts

genetic engineering: cutting up and combining genetic material from two different species in order to produce certain traits in a new plant or animal

geometric: based on simple shapes like circles, lines, or squares

GPS: a Global Positioning System, used to find a location

hover: to hang in the air for a period of time

humidity: the level of moisture in the air

hype: excessive promotion or publicity

marvel: something that inspires surprise and amazement

NASA: the National Aeronautics and Space Administration

nocturnal: active mostly at night

odometer: a device that measures a distance traveled

ordeal: a difficult or unpleasant experience

peak: the highest point

psychosis: a mental condition in which a person cannot tell what is real from what is not

radiation: energy put off in waves or particles

sacred: something that is respected for being holy or used to pray to a god or gods

saucer: a small plate

satellite: an object or vehicle made to orbit the Earth or moon

scorch: to burn a surface to the point that its color and texture change

UFO: an Unidentified Flying Object

uncanny: something that feels mysterious or supernatural

Quiz

How many shapes have been found in the Nazca desert?

Answer: 300

When did alien abductions begin to be reported?

Answer: The 1800s

Where are most crop circles found?

Answer: Great Britain

What year did hundreds of people report seeing V-shaped lights in Arizona and New Mexico?

Answer: 1997

When did the first crop circles begin appearing?

Answer: 1600s

How many times a day are weather balloons sent up into the atmosphere?

Answer: Twice

INDEX

SELECTED BIBLIOGRAPHY

"Ancient Alien Theory." *History.com.* Accessed February 6, 2017. http:// css.history.com/shows/ancient-aliens/articles/ancient-alien-theory.

Angelo, Joseph A. *The Extraterrestrial Encyclopedia: Our Search for Life in Outer Space.* New York, NY: Facts on File Publications, 1985.

Blevins, Jason. "Cow Mutilations Baffle Ranchers, Cops, UFO Believer." *The Denver Post.* December 8, 2009. Web. Accessed February 6, 2017. http://www.denverpost. com/2009/12/08/colorado-cow-mutilations-baffle-ranchers-cops-ufo-believer/.

Fitzgerald, Randall. *The Complete Book of Extraterrestrial Encounters.* New York, NY: Macmillan Publishing Group Co., Inc., 1979.

Kuzoian, Alex. "40 Years Ago, NASA Sent a Message to Aliens—Here's What It Says." *Business Insider.* February 17, 2016. Web. Accessed February 6, 2017. http://www. businessinsider.com/voyagers-golden-record-nasa-message-aliens-2016-2.

Radford, Benjamin. "Crop Circles Explained." *Live Science.* January 23, 2013. Web. Accessed February 6, 2017. http://www.livescience.com/26540-crop-circles.html.

Speigel, Lee. "UFO-Alien Abduction Still Haunts Travis Walton." *The Huffington Post.* April 23, 2015. Web. Accessed February 6, 2017. http://www.huffingtonpost. com/2015/04/23/travis-walton-still-haunted-by-ufo_n_7119910.html.

Wolchover, Natalie. "The Surprising Origin of Alien Abduction Stories." *Live Science.* May 11, 2012. Web. Accessed February 6, 2017. http:// www.livescience.com/20250-alien-abductions-origins.html.